I WRITE
in the dark

my truth be told

REVIEWS & ENCOURAGEMENTS

My grandma Kat has been waiting for this moment. I am writing this note to show appreciation. She has tried so hard to accomplish this book. I am most proud of her for finishing so it can be presented to the world. I am proud that my grandma has accomplished so much in life.

PS ~ Grandma, you are never too old to do anything you want to do!

Kevion
(Felecia's 10 year-old grandson)

Felecia, you are an inspiration and I will always cherish the genuine person you are. "I WRITE in the dark" is a read that can be a self-help to many people who have been through hard times in life and need the encouragement to keep going. It goes straight to the heart and then to the mind. The poetry in this book has great energy too. After knowing you for eleven years I am not surprised that you have written such an upfront, honest book that will encourage many.

Danielle Cameron
Senior Customer Service Agent and Friend

I commend Felecia for exposing her personnel life to help someone who may have traveled or who is traveling the same road. Many times as Christians we love to testify of our successes in life. For some reason we want to omit our utter failures, not realizing that our failures played a major role in who we are today. When we survey our lives, the good, the bad and the ugly we realize that these were the things which contributed to our uniqueness. I pray that this book will allow Christians to be willing to expose themselves for the glory of God!

Elder Fred J. Pervine Jr.

I WRITE
in the dark

my truth be told

Felecia Marie Wellington

WELLINGTON
Literary Works

INDIANAPOLIS, IN

I WRITE in the dark
My Truth Be Told
Felecia Wellington

ISBN-13: 978-1503207813
Library of Congress Control Number: 2015915221

PUBLISHED BY
Wellington Literary Works
Indianapolis, IN
wellingtonliterary@yahoo.com

Unless otherwise noted, all Scripture quotations are from
THE KING JAMES VERSION of the Holy Bible.

This book is manufactured in the United States of America.

~~~~~~

Developmental Editor:
Elaine Leonard

Project Manager, Cover and Interior Designer:
Annie Gonzales

Author Photograph:
Kysha La-Faye
La-Faye Photography

DEDICATION

I dedicate my book to my phenomenal children, Erik'ka and Michael, and to my wonderful grandchildren, Kevion, Billie, and Ayce.

My prayer to God is that by sharing this book you will understand me more and some of the trials I experienced; that you know you are more than capable to accomplish great things; to appreciate yourselves for the awesome and amazing blessings that you are to the world! I want you to know that I carry a great amount of gratitude for being blessed with you. Each of you has experienced what is called a testimony. Your lives are full of God's greatness and displays His miracles beyond anything that I could have ever done to make your lives better.

My request to you is that you live freely, happy, without fears and without hesitation. Encourage your children to take chances, and to not be afraid to be imperfect. Let go of what hurts and create new memories! Appreciate and always be available for each other.

Don't ever give up! You are victorious!!! Let God lead you so that you don't get lost. I'M VERY PROUD OF YOU! I LOVE YOU!

ACKNOWLEDGMENTS

Life isn't always easy, but how fortunate we are when God plants people around us to help us make it through; people who help to keep us encouraged and remind us that we are capable. Through this experience I have used writing as therapy and have truly learned a lot about myself, as well as others. We each need each other. I am grateful for every lesson, both good and bad, because they all are a part of who I am today.

I've been touched by so many in a variety of ways, and I say thank you to all of you. I'd like to personally acknowledge those few who, no matter the place I was in, were always present. I would like to acknowledge the words, late night calls, listening without judging and most importantly, helping to keep me focused on the true purpose assigned to me.

Thank you to my awesome big brothers Tony and Mikey. I understand much better the love you have for me and I am grateful to have you in my life.

My dear beautiful Mary Ann, I say thank you for being my sister without condition. You just loved me no matter what. I thank you.

To my amazing cousin Charonda, where do I start? Thank you for countless years of your unselfish presence. You never say no; you never stop helping.

To my technical helper Joshua Vitalis who answered calls for help when I felt overwhelmed with the computer. He'd laugh and say "keep going". Thank you.

To Rikki, my beautiful amazing daughter. She doesn't say much, but when she speaks it's powerful and I am encouraged by her strong presence. How blessed I am to have you! I love you! Greater things are coming to your life, for sure.

My miracle son, Mikey. Wow, thank you for being my son and enduring such an occurrence. The near loss of your life is the reason my life began. You are so strong, son!

Thank you to the wonderful people God sent my way to help complete this assignment; Faith McKinney (mentor), Elaine Leonard (developmental editor), Annie Gonzales (cover and interior designer) and Kysha La-Faye (Lafaye Photography) for helping me to fulfill this accomplishment. How perfect the timing was that you entered my life!

Thank you isn't enough sometimes, but being grateful is sufficient. I AM GRATEFUL for each and every one of you!

To my readers: appreciate the people God sends to you because they are on assignment too. Everyone matters!

CONTENTS

FOREWORD

Felecia's book, "I WRITE in the dark", chronicles her life's journey. She has a keen grasp on the written word which allows the reader insight into the choices made, which ultimately impacted her emotionally. This beautiful woman endured successes, failures, pain and great joys, which she is able to articulate through written prose, as well as adding a sense of poetic flair. Readers will enjoy and be enriched by Ms. Wellington's story.

Having been acquainted with Felecia for over 20 years, I was amazed and enlightened by many deep-rooted experiences that contributed to her multi-dimensional outlook. You will find when reading her book, each of us has much in common, yet it's our experiences that make us equally distanced. This book should be shared by those seeking growth and development, but are afraid to open those doors and turn on the lights.

MaryAnn Endsley-Williams
H.R Advisor and Friend

PREFACE

WELCOME TO MY DISORDER...as you read my book you will find that there appears to be no order to how I write. I write according to the moments I am experiencing and unfortunately, most of those moments have no apparent order. I don't write to explain. I write to express. It's for my own understanding, so that I can have some type of order in the midst of my DISORDER. So please follow me as I write my way through my DISORDER...to a new life.

INTRODUCTION

Give me a pen and paper and I'll write. I never write to read; I mostly write to express how I'm feeling at that moment. I've written poetry most of my life and most of the time I find answers to my own questions – like, what makes me doubt myself? How can such a strong person have so many fears? And how can I be so blessed and feel so broken at the same time?

It wasn't long after the accident that God put the title of my book, "I WRITE in the dark", in my heart. I found myself wondering if when people read it how many of them would find that they have been in the dark too. But no matter what cycle of life I was in I knew one thing for sure. I knew that I had to keep trusting God for my survival through all of the things that could have easily been my demise, my default, and the disappearance of my own self without anyone even noticing that I had gone away.

A spirit that's loose, no presence to see.
A broken soul reaching, but no one sees me.

"I WRITE in the dark" because that is truly when I write. Either I'm going through a dark moment or I'm awake in the middle of a dark night with my pen and paper … writing.

My feelings aren't easily dismissed because I search for reasons why, trying to figure things out. I want to understand others because I feel misunderstood myself. It's kind of funny how when I was younger I never paid much attention to people or what was going on around me. Now it appears that God has me paying attention to everyone and everything, because I don't want anyone to feel dismissed.

> *What is your weakness could also be your strength.*
> *But be careful not to get caught in the middle,*
> *'cause you could find your SELF lost there.*

Every step of the way I know it was God that guided me through and for that I am thankful!

PART 1

THE TRUTH about my darkness

Pen and Paper

Any given night I may wake up out of sleep and grab for the pen and paper that I keep by my bed. I also keep a pen and paper in my purse. Anywhere I go you can be sure that I have a pen and paper with me. In a split second I can have a thought, a few words that I don't want to forget. Like the myriad of writings on pieces of papers I've stored away, I am gathering my thoughts like trying to put a puzzle together, trying to put myself together. I'm going to pray my way through all of the pieces while I peace myself together.

You will see that I speak about God a lot. Truly, He is the director of my journey. Even in the times when I felt alone, my heart knew that I wasn't. No matter what my mind tried to convince me of, I knew He was there. I always wanted to be pleasing to God to be honest, but I also thought that God was so disappointed in me that my good intentions or desires to do good didn't matter. It seemed that my guilt was greater than my appreciation of just how blessed I really was; that perfection was a place that didn't exist at all. I thought my imperfections made me the person I was, who I am, and who I am supposed to be. And that God had a plan for my life, a purpose for my trials, and a reason for my seasons of tests.

Is it me or does anyone else find themselves searching for themselves? That may sound funny to a few of you, but I'm sure it won't be the last thing that makes you laugh moving forward. Keep in mind that I am only speaking about MY truths, the truth about how I really feel and how my feelings either helped me or hurt me in this process of becoming who God intended me to be. I can honestly say I should have given up a long time ago, but God had other plans!

Mercy and grace over me is the reason why I didn't give up on life. Yes, God was there to guide me!

...strength can become one's weakness
if at any point the strength becomes broken...

Religion and Me

It took me a long time to understand that religion is not necessarily God. You see, I was comfortable living as I was, without explanations. I had gotten closer to the devil, who had no expectations of me or how I was living, so it was easy not thinking about God. You see, I always believed, but I stopped seeking. Even when my mind was influenced by defeat, He kept me safe and I knew it.

I tried going to church several times and for some reason could never find the connection I was looking for or needed. Watching others serve God was a distraction and a disappointment. It made me want to stop going to church, because it seemed like there was not much difference between those who practiced religion faithfully and me.

I remember horrible nights of loneliness, hopelessness, depression, and heartache. There were many drunken staggering nights out in the streets appearing to be having fun, but in reality I was searching for a simple sign from a God I had no relationship with. I was hoping He would let me know that at some point my heart's pain would stop, my spirit would grow and, that most of all, I would change. Yes, I was desperately hanging on to the hope that my life could somehow become different.

I knew things inside of me were broken because I had allowed my soul to be traded for destruction. I was definitely fighting a losing battle. The older I got the easier it became for me to hide how I was feeling. I appeared strong, but strength can become one's weakness if at any point the strength becomes broken, and broken I was.

I wanted to belong to something, so I went to churches wanting to fit in. I wanted the people to notice that regardless of how I looked on the outside I needed help, but no one seemed to notice. Like the rest of my life, even my Christian testimony was for someone else's benefit. It became more important to me that I follow the desires of their hearts instead of God's. I don't know what was more hurtful, the church people not noticing or the people in my daily life not knowing that I desperately needed help. To this day I have allowed the disappointment of being overlooked by people keep me away from church. However, it has not kept me from trying to serve God the best I can. I do believe that since God knows everything I no longer have to try to prove myself or prove my purpose to anyone – and it's actually a pretty good feeling. Just being able to write this book is proof to me that He has kept me close! I understand now that people are not perfect and it's my relationship with God that really matters.

I understand now that people are not perfect and it's my relationship with God that really matters.

The Accident

How can something happen in a clock's tick that turns your life upside down? It was on June 25, 2005 at 9:31pm, that my life was changed forever! I was supposed to be meeting a friend at a club I usually frequented after work and on weekends, but I wasn't feeling well. Mikey, my 18 year old son, came in the door with his then 6 month old son Kevi and asked if I was leaving. When I told him I was sick, he said he was going to leave my grandson with me while he went to get some food. I agreed, and he said he would be right back. It took only 5 minutes for devastation to begin.

Knock! Knock!

I was struck with terror and alarm, *"Who is it?"*

"It's me from next door!"

When I opened the door standing there was my 12 year old neighbor, *"Your son has been hit!"*

Stunned I replied, *"Huh?"*

He repeated, *"Your son has been hit! It's Mikey! He's been in a bad accident!"*

My mind was a blur. I couldn't grasp what he was talking about. I turned to look at my grandson and noticed the time. It was 9:31pm. I remember hearing my name repeatedly, *"Kat, Kat,"* but I had started screaming. Afraid of the unknown, I remember thinking life was never going to be the same again; that something dreadful had happened that would change our lives forever. This was the beginning of the worse night of my life – yet the turning point to transformation!

I was still screaming now – uncontrollably. The thought of death was consuming me. My next-door neighbor came rushing through the door. I just kept screaming. Everything was loud, so loud; everything in my head was so very loud! I remember a feeling of death flowing through my veins, flowing through my thoughts, flowing through me. I felt as if life was over.

My neighbor somehow got me in her car and before we could get around the corner I noticed flashing lights. There were so many bright lights. I couldn't get myself together. As we got closer, I saw fire trucks, police cars, ambulances, and people; so many people, so many, many people. I literally opened the car door and jumped out to run to the scene of my nightmare, but I fell on my knees because the car was still moving. I thought I'd never get to my son in time. I had to run to my son! When I got up all I saw was a huge red blanket tossed into the air. I thought it meant my son was dead. I was suddenly reminded of a movie that I had seen with a horrible accident scene. I remember the red blanket in that movie was to cover up death. That red blanket will probably be in my mind forever.

I heard people calling my name while I was still running and then all of a sudden I felt like I had been transported to another place. I was running but I felt like I was stuck in place, a dark place. My feet were moving but I wasn't getting closer. I felt so very alone while I was anxiously and desperately seeking for my son. I started looking for my daughter Rikki too, because I knew she was the one person who could help me.

At this time in my life I was friends with several firefighters. The next thing I knew one of those firefighters came to me and said they would get my son out of the car, but I still didn't see his car. I was screaming my son's name hoping that this was all a big mistake. I was hoping that I had been misplaced into the wrong nightmare. I felt like my darkness had turned even darker. Then I felt a sensation of being invisible come over me. That feeling made me scream louder and louder. I was gasping for air. I couldn't breathe and just fell to the ground. I wanted to die, but had an asthma attack instead. The medic rushed to my side to give me oxygen, but all I wanted was to know where my son was.

I could hear my daughter's voice saying, *"Mama, please! Please mama!"* Hearing her voice gave me strength.

I got up off the ground and then heard another voice say, *"We got him!"*

I started running when someone grabbed me and stopped me. I saw the firefighters with my son pushing him up the hill on a gurney. As they got closer, I remember my heart was racing, my head was pounding, and I was still gasping for air. He's still alive! I heard them say, *"He's alive!"* Just that fast I saw my son, my dying son.

My daughter made the decision to have him transported to Methodist Hospital. He was in the ambulance now so my daughter and her friend got me in the car. As we followed the ambulance to the hospital, I remember thinking, *"He doesn't even know we are here for him."*

I felt cold. I felt angry. What if he doesn't make it? The blinding lights from the ambulance and the police cars were all I could see. It seemed like an eternity before we got to the hospital.

My daughter was crying, saying, *"Please don't let him die! Please don't let my brother die!"*

My son had coded blue several times in the ambulance so I was unable to see him right away as they took him out and into the hospital. Blood was everywhere. For just that moment, as I got a glance of my son, blood was all I saw. People were doing their best to calm me down, but I was in such disbelief that I was numb. My hearing was muted. My voice became silent. I was detached from reality. Chaplains started coming to talk to me. I would curse and scream at them because I thought they were coming to tell me my son had died, but God had someone on special assignment for me that night!

A lady chaplain came to talk to me and, when she walked into the waiting room at the hospital, I felt a sense of quiet come over me. She said, *"Felecia, your son needs you to pray right now."* She took me to a corner and told me to talk to God. She told me that my son was still alive and that there was power in my prayers. She told me that God was waiting on me to pray so that He could help my son.

All of a sudden, I went from cursing to screaming, from screaming to silence. Finally, I realized that I needed to go to God; that I needed to pray for my son no matter how I felt because he was still alive. He needed me to do my part as his mother and pray. And pray I did!

I asked forgiveness for making such a mockery out of my life, for ignoring the call to worship God and for not showing gratitude. I also asked forgiveness for not loving myself properly, for not loving my children properly, and for not loving life for the blessing that it was. Before I knew it I was in His presence. God let me know He was listening to me. When I finished praying the chaplain told me she had to call her husband to alert him of her late arrival home due to the number of people who were there waiting for updates on my son.

It was a long weary night. My stomach ached and my head hurt. I kept thinking, "Ok, now what? I've prayed. What next, God?"

I kept hearing the loud crashing sound of the accident's impact in my head even though I wasn't there when it happened. It was a horrible sound that kept repeating itself and plagued me for years. I found myself waiting in this spiral of confusion and doubt, wondering if God would come through for me. I kept thinking that my prayer was too late, but thanks to Jesus, the morning told me otherwise – my son made it through the night!

Then I started to hear of the many ways God had been aligning things up for our miracle. The Chaplain from the night before came and asked me where my son worked. She said when she got home she told her husband about the horrible accident only to find out that my son and her husband not only worked together, but were good friends. As we continued talking the Chaplain shared with me that her husband had been alerted to my son's accident while at work and that a prayer had been said by him and the other employees. On this particular night God had positioned these pastors, a husband and wife, to take care of us, not knowing that they would separately be praying for the same mother and son in need of prayer. She continued to stay with me and even check on me periodically giving me much needed support. I will never forget what her and her husband did. They helped me find my way to prayer.

Even in my darkest fears I prayed!

The Long Recovery

Though my son made it through the night he suffered many injuries: head trauma, broken bones, skull fractures, and a shattered pelvic. The impact also sliced the muscle that controls the jaw so facial palsy was a result with no definite procedure to fix it. The doctors tried to come up with ideas or possible surgeries to correct it, but none seemed to be the answer. His mouth was left hanging open by about 7 inches without the ability to close because there was no muscle there to control it. His tear duct was also damaged. I was advised that my son would never cry again but that seemed minor. I just wanted my son to live no matter what injuries he had. I just wanted him to live!

Several days went by, waiting. Several nights went by, waiting, because that's all I could do. Every night for weeks the doctors said they weren't sure if my son would make it through the night. Weeks turned into months, but I kept reminding myself to pray. Even in my darkest fears I prayed!

He had a temperature of 103 for so long that the doctors said if it didn't go away it could be what killed him. That didn't even include all of the trauma he had sustained. They put him on a bed that had the ability to change temperatures. They kept the bed freezing to help keep my son's temperature down and his body stable.

Nights and more nights went by, praying. I was still praying. I was praying to a God I had never really spent time with before and hoping that He would somehow see fit to forgive me for living so poorly and for not reaching out to Him sooner. I knew that even in all the despair I was in, that somehow this would be the thing that changed my life. This would be the one time that would always and forever be etched into my heart. Somehow I needed to find the strength and courage to trust God for what I didn't even know.

Months had gone by and Mikey was hanging on, but there were still lots of complications. His temperature was going up and down. X-rays were taken and they found that there were spots on his brain, as well as bruising. They were unsure if the spots would create any type of brain restrictions or dysfunction. Yet through it all I was still waiting for God to perform a miracle.

One day the doctor came into the waiting room while I was resting. When I looked up he was standing in front of me and my first thought was *"Oh no! Not bad news, please no!"*

He said, *"We examined your son this morning and the spots on his brain are gone."*

I started screaming! God was beginning to show me the miracle I was seeking, but even with this good news I was still doubtful. Mikey had several broken ribs, a shattered pelvic bone, and a broken collarbone, so I went back to waiting. Waiting again.

My daughter took care of me during this time like I was her child. Whenever I saw her face I knew I had to pull myself together, even though I wasn't always great at it. I had been at the hospital for days when I decided that I wasn't going to leave my son. In my heart I felt that if I left his side I would lose him. I felt so guilty. I thought everything was my fault, so I had to stay there no matter what. I never even stepped out the door of the hospital for 6 months because I was afraid something might happen to my son. It was truly the presence of my daughter and her strength that pushed me through. She took on so many responsibilities and was there to make sure I had everything I needed to stay by her brother's side.

At that time the house I was living in was not important to me anymore. I told my daughter that I wasn't going to go back to that house; life was over for me there. She arranged for things to be packed up and moved out. I cannot express all my gratitude to my daughter and brothers for all they did to help. For a very long time she took care of me.

There were lots of people coming to pray for my son every day, all

*I knew that even in all the despair I was in,
that somehow this would be the thing that changed my life...
Somehow I needed to find the strength and courage to trust
God for what I didn't even know.*

day. Some of these people were strangers to me but I felt so much better when I heard the pitter-patter of walking feet because I knew someone was there to pray for my son and me. They had exactly what I needed to survive the season I was in – whether it was food, prayer, a hug, or an encouraging word, they were there. I will never forget what they did, and I will never forget how they blessed me for all of those days.

At this time, though things were still touch and go, my son was not out of danger yet. One morning, when I woke up, I was asked to go to a meeting with the surgeon. He had previously said that surgery for Mikey's broken bones was needed as soon as possible. However, whenever it was time to prepare him for surgery, they would tell me it was postponed because his condition was so poor.

I was going through this spiral again of doubt, hating myself, and blaming myself for the accident. So much was circling in my head I thought I'd go crazy. At one point I actually wanted to die, because I was so weak. I had convinced myself that I was the cause of this horrible thing, this dark ugly disaster. I thought I had brought all of this on my son, my grandson, and my daughter. My life seemed useless to me at that moment, but someone had to be praying for me, because I continued on!

I was extremely low when I went to the meeting with the surgeon and team of doctors – expecting the worse. To my surprise I was told, *"Ms. Wellington, we have no explanation for the changes that have taken place overnight with Michael. All we can tell you is that the surgery is not needed at this time because his bones are mending."*

I remember the look on their faces was as if they were in disbelief, just as I was. I fell to my knees screaming and they just let me scream. I think they wanted to scream too. Yes, broken collarbone, shattered pelvic, several broken ribs, multiple skull fractures, and the spots on the brain were all healed! Not one surgery was needed!

After aggressive research, it was found that broken bones had splintered into my son's internal cavities causing the temperature. This was allowing blood and fluids to hide in pockets creating this horrible fever for weeks and weeks. Doctors arranged to insert little grenade-like objects into both of his sides. In a matter of days the fluids started to pour out. Gallons of blood and puss began to flow out of him. He was being cleansed.

Thank you Lord Jesus! I still cry! I still shout! I still live through it and to be honest, I need to remember so that I never forget what God has done for my son and me! Thank you Lord! Thank you!

Just as soon as the miracle happened though, Mikey took a bad turn. Late night medications were distributed to my son one evening. It wasn't until the next morning that I discovered something terribly wrong had happened. I remember as if it were yesterday waking up next to his bed and seeing him in a fetal position with his eyes fixed straight ahead. I knew something had gone wrong. I screamed for someone to come and help him.

Mikey had been given the wrong medicine, which caused him to have a stroke and be placed back into ICU for two more weeks. With the aid of Benadryl disposed into his blood, doctors were able to reverse the condition caused by improper medication given to him. It was later determined that he had been given Haldo, a medicine given to people with schizophrenia, which can cause hallucinations and strokes.

After much pain and doubt, Mikey made it to his recovery. God had been there through it all! With the exception of a slight facial palsy and not being able to cry because of torn tear ducts, my son recovered completely after leaving the hospital and months in rehab and outpatient visits. After 2 years he was finally released from everything to go back to normal living. He returned to work, bought a home and continued raising his son. Mikey truly is a walking miracle!

I, on the other hand, wasn't sure how to restart my life now.

About Me

I had given up everything to be by my son's side through his re-covery and I knew I had to start over now. I felt as if God had taken His arm and knocked everything off my table, cleaned my slate, and rebirthed me again. I later understood that in order for me to reach the goal of being a better me, a recovered me, a changed me, I had to start life over, from the bottom, leaving the old and painful past behind. I also knew I was going to have to cleanup some things in order to reach restoration.

Before the accident, I was in a relationship with a drug dealer and at the time I thought I was controlling the course of the relationship. However, I quickly found out that I wasn't. I would take money and use sex to get what I wanted from him, selling my soul to the devil, and trading myself for things of no value because I felt so worthless.

While we were having sex one day, I told him that I didn't want to continue the relationship. For some silly reason I thought it would be the perfect timing to cut him loose. The relationship had gotten out of control. He was stalking me and had made several threats to do me harm if I ever stopped seeing him. Every time I thought I had the control to leave, he'd threaten me, so I continued to see him and take his money.

Eventually though I got a restraining order and decided to get a permit and gun. When the restraining order was served to him he came to my home and tore it up while telling me that he would never leave me alone. I was definitely afraid after that. I knew things were so out of control that something was sure to happen. I was used to being strong and independent and didn't feel like I had anyone to go to. I truly needed help figuring this one out. The only place I knew to go was God, so I asked Him to remove him from my life. Things were getting even worse. He was following me everywhere I went.

In the meantime I had been clubbing, drinking and doing things that kept me distracted from the reality that my life was totally destructive. My main thing to do was get dressed, fix myself up, and hit the streets. It became a cycle for me to go to work, club, go to the after-hour club, and then have sex, which became my greatest addiction. I used sex to get what I wanted, though I didn't even know what I really wanted at the time. Sex and drinking gave me a moment of pleasure and satisfaction, but it didn't give me the love I was truly seeking.

I was a sex addict. Yes, that's right. *"Hi, my name is Felecia and I am a recovering sex addict."* I was having sex multiple times a day, with multiple men, each encounter pushing my soul further and further into self-destruction. It didn't matter where I was. I would have sex, even in public places, if that was the mood I was in. There were times I would vomit afterwards because I couldn't stand the smell of sex, but it didn't stop me. I hated myself so much for lying on my back, under him, on top of him, any way I could get it, because my heart never knew love.

What I did know though was that I wanted this crazy man out of my life. I wanted control of my life back. I felt like he was totally out of control so I needed him to go away. I continued my broken prayers. I say broken because I wasn't worshipping God, and I had this feeling that because of that I wasn't on God's priority list.

However, one day came that allowed me to be free of him. The phone rang and I was told that a shooting had taken place. Later I found out that this guy who I wanted away from me had been out with another woman. He had been shot 10 times in the midst of a robbery gone wrong and had a long recovery after that. All I knew was that I was finally free.

After that situation I told myself that I never wanted to have sex again. I was afraid that sex would recreate this encounter all over again, but I couldn't stop. I knew I had to change, but I didn't want to be-cause I was familiar with my lifestyle. I continued hanging out, hooking up, and putting myself at risk. It's funny how things happen to us that should be opportunities for us to change but we don't take it. On top of that we keep so many secrets inside that no one really knows us or how to help us.

In the midst of this I was trying to be a good mom. I had figured out that I had serious issues and sex was just one of them. I had low self-esteem, but, because I was strong, it didn't look like it. I would fit in no matter the environment I was in so no one knew my problems. Somehow, I managed to get my children through school and keep them off drugs and alcohol, even though I allowed those things to be around them. They were great children, even though I wasted a lot of time being away from them.

We often say if I could go back, but if I went back and changed anything I would change the ways I expected from others and the ways I didn't expect from myself. I know that I am loved but I felt loveless most of the time. Still to this day there is something inside of me that isn't fulfilled. If I ever look back over my life there is one person who I desired love from the most, but always felt separated from, and that is my mom. While writing this book I am learning the importance of understanding. While I am remembering my story, she is remembering hers too. I realize that she has struggled through things; that she may also have reminders of yesterday secretly hiding in her soul too. What I understand is that we both need to be present to help each other survive and be able to move forward.

Though our relationship has struggled over the years, I am grateful for my mother. I understand that we can't erase the past but we can change the course of the future for generations to come if we allow our hearts to mend. If I could go back and change time, I would definitely be more present for her. But it's not too late because we are still here and we have a chance to get it right.

I love you Momma. I did my best and I know that you did too.
I am you and you are me. God is allowing us a season for mending,
a season for restoration and I am excited about that!

If it had not been for this upset happening in my life – this unplanned moment of despair – I believe my life would have withered away. I truly understand that after this experience I was given another chance – that God was showing favor over my son's life and mine. I understand that this was the beginning to a new life for us. Restoration and pursuit of a new me was just beginning! God's mercy and grace was definitely at work and I was ready to change. I often say, *"WOW! How fortunate I am to have this life changing opportunity and we survived it!"* I thought, *"How special I must be to God to receive such a gift...a second chance at life!"* I knew I couldn't let God down, I was ready for His will to be done.

I encourage anyone who is experiencing hardship of any kind –trust God! It isn't always an easy process – changing, leaving old things that bind us, removing people from our lives, changing the places we go to. No, it isn't easy, but it IS worth it! I went through a period of seclusion, but it is what I needed to stay focused on God's will for me. From my heart I say to you, trust God through your unknown and once you get your feet moving in the way of His plans life will be a lot easier for you! It wont be perfect, but it will be easier.

Trust God through your unknown and once you get your feet moving in the way of His plans life will be a lot easier for you!

PART 2

POETRY...LIGHT in the darkness

My Writing

I used to write when I was in grade school. My dad and others would always tell me I should keep writing, but I got away from it because I got older and stopped living. I didn't have much to write about any more.

It has only been since the accident that I started writing again. As I wrote I started experiencing my own true story of mercy and grace right before my eyes. Yes, my own miracle was taking place!

In this section I am going to share some of my poetry with you about how I feel on the inside. I like poetry because you can put words to your feelings, how you look at things, and what lies inside your heart. It's a funny thing because expressions don't always match what we see. I have found out that I am good at covering things up, but in doing so I am creating my own pain as well. When I cover up I forget what I need to fix or what has hurt me. It seems that those things that I need to let go of just go way back to the back of my mind to hide out and in moments without notice will come up for recycling. It's at those moments when I write the words that fit my situation. The thoughts are my harvest on the inside.

I hope that what I write might be the words that someone else has on the inside too. It's been like therapy for me. I hope it's therapy for you too... to make it through bad days. To help you through days when you feel like giving up. To help you through days when you feel like no one is there for you. To help you through days when you feel like not even God is there. I pray that reading them would be like a word of encouragement, an ear of understanding, a hug, and hope from the dark.

For me there were times when I just wanted someone to notice, someone to see that I was not as strong as I appeared to be. How can I be broken to pieces and no one see the cracks? As I'm sitting here I'm remembering times when I went to others hoping that they would just give me a hug or a word of encouragement. That they would take a minute to talk with me even if understanding wasn't achieved. It was then that I would write. So as you read further please try not to judge me, but remember I was writing in the dark...and hopefully it will help you see and get a glimpse of light.

Depression

Depression...dark places that the mind travels to.
Trying to keep it secret that I am battling with myself.
Trying to keep it together while I am falling apart.
Smiling to cover up the pain because the feeling of failure
won't let me be honest in front of others.
But no one notices the truth anyway.
No one notices that I'm in the dark.
But maybe, just maybe, those around me are in the dark too.
Maybe that's why they don't see me?
So somehow I manage to keep smiling and be as present as I can be,
So that while others are missing me...
I am not missing myself!

Look for ME!

Here, but not present
Drifting away
In need of a rescue
'cuz my self has gone astray.

Who wants to talk about depression? Afraid of being ridiculed, laughed at, or even questioned about how you got into this place. It's a feeling of remorse because somehow you lost yourself. No one understands and they pretend to not notice because with acknowledgement comes responsibility.

How lucky am I that I eventually found someone to talk to; someone noticed me! *Thank you, Lord, for noticing and listening to me!*

Being Strong

Being strong is a complicated thing.
Nobody even notices
When you scream.
You count on yourself
To put it all together
And nobody sees that you're stuck in bad weather.

So who do you go to
When your strong isn't enough?
And those around you watching
Expect you to be tough.
Being strong is a funny thing.
Nobody notices when you scream.

I'm so used to being strong I wish I knew how not to be...
sometimes strong can be weak.

So, who do I go to when I need strength to carry on?

"He gives strength to the weary and increases the power of the weak.
Even youths grow tired and weary, and young men stumble and fall;
but those who hope in the Lord will renew their strength.
They will soar on wings like eagles;
they will run and not grow weary, they will walk and not be faint."

Isaiah 40:29-31 (NIV)

Fly Away

What we see with our eyes
We record with our minds.
When our vision goes dark
Memories help us to find
Ourselves.

Don't fly away too far
Your self is needed here.
Recreate what you remember.
Fly back to yourself
Without fear.

Thank you Lord for spreading my wings...
I am finally flying in the right direction!

Pain

What I have found through my own life experiences is that I hurt.
I hurt in my heart about the past.
I hurt about things I wish I could change.
I hurt about not being able to forget those things that hurt in order to move forward.
Mostly I hurt because I can never seem to fully forgive myself for mistakes I've made in the past and that I still make today.

My pain comes from expectations.
My pain comes from feeling alone.
My pain comes from fear of failure.
My pain comes from fear of success.
My pain comes from a place in my heart that I just can't seem to repair.
It has become a part of me and my lifestyle.
I have gotten comfortable with my pain, but
today I have decided to try something new.

I have decided to try and live without my pain…
I don't need it anymore!

I know now that living with pain is not a part of my purpose. I understand that God's plans for my life include happiness and joy. The acceptance of painful things that exist in our lives must go away. In order for us to receive God's will we must be willing to follow Gods plans for our purpose and let go of what hurts.

I truly get it now – I *can* do it with God's help!

The Pain Inside

I feel very sad that the world, many times, isn't open to discuss the things that hurt us. We put on costumes to hide from our realities in order to fit in while we are suffering. Why is it that way?

Some of the pains we encounter in life come from past generational bondages. Our pasts effect our present if we don't release them. We have tendencies to backpack them around like priceless treasures when we know inside of us that it's just priceless junk without value. Depressions, illnesses, anxieties, fears, and all of the other crippling diseases that suffocate the heart and stop it from beating, stop us from living.

Why is it that we expect so much from each other? Why is it that we don't trust each other? Why is it that we'd rather suffer alone than to hopefully find resolutions? Everyone says we should pray together but we still pray alone.

At some point, there is a place inside of us that we must visit – that painful place that reaches out and destroys our happiness. At some point, we have to trust each other enough to help us survive what could possibly be our demise.

Pain kills...will you notice it when it comes your way? Will you notice when someone is in need of your help if they come your way?

I Declare

What I miss within myself I am promising to rebuild and not be my own defeat. I have to love myself more. Appreciate myself more. Support myself more. Love others more. Appreciate others more. Try to show an example to my children and grandchildren of the importance of loving themselves unconditionally so that their lives are fulfilled and happy. To demonstrate to those around me that I can conquer the one thing that seems to be the hardest for me...SELF.

There are people in my life that I wished loved me more, but not to just say it or expect me to know it. I wish they knew the impact of saying they loved me but forgetting to show me. Forgetting to wrap their arms around me and truly letting me know that I was loved. So I declare to love differently. I declare to love myself more, so that I can love others rightly.

What do you declare today? What changes can you make that impact others? What can you give to others that was not given to you?

When you know that the one thing you are missing in your life is the same thing that's going to help you to your victory and may help those you love get to their victory too, then how can you withhold it?

Back Home

What's the hurry
To leave the house
In such a rush to see
What the streets are all about?

But now I can't wait
To get back home.
If it wasn't for God
I would have died
In the streets alone.

I left home way too soon, searching for a lot of things, but all I found was that I lost myself in the process. It takes years to recover what's lost, especially when you don't even know that it's missing.

I'm glad I found my way back home.

A Part of Me

A part of me is dead.
Can't find my thoughts
Inside of my head,
But my pen doesn't need
What's inside my head.
It needs me to write
What's in my heart instead.

Sometimes I go searching for my thoughts because, if for one moment they are not there, I start to think that I am incomplete. I'm used to having so much on my mind. It's funny that the thought of not having anything to write about frightens me. But I'm learning that there is always a reason to write and it's ok that I don't have to search very far to find it.

A Conversation with Two

Today I asked GOD,
"Why should I serve you?"
I got an answer from the devil that he's the one who always sees me through.
But then GOD said, "Remember the times you wanted to quit?"
*And the devil replied, "Yea, but why is she always going through bull**?"*
Then God reminded me that He has the power to save my soul.
Yet the devil replied, "Then why is her heart always so full of sorrow?"
God said, "Felecia, keep your head up. Stand strong and pray."
Then the devil reminded me that I'm struggling alone yet another day.
But I decided to pray and I prayed! And I prayed!
Up ahead the devil's there standing, blocking my prayers away,
So I keep asking myself, "Is it really worth it to serve?
Cause the battle of heaven and hell is getting on my nerves."
Somehow through this battle
There is one thing I can see
And it is that GOD was still present with me,
And that no matter the battle I was in
GOD was there again and again.
So I made the decision
To keep God in my life
No matter the devil's visits
Turning my days into dark nights.

Hardest battle I ever had was simple...to just trust God no matter what the devil said.

Broken Pieces

Broken pieces
Scattered around,
Like falling leaves
Blowing to the ground.
The pieces make a puzzle
A beautiful picture, you see.
Like deep rooted seeds
Growing like branches on a tree.
So when you look at the pieces,
Look again, you will see
The tree that is standing
Is me on my feet!

Lord, please grow me into the woman that you have plans for me to be!
I am reaching out to YOU.

Broken

Because living differently
Creates different visions
Of what we see,
Pain and joy, hurt and brokenness
Can forever be remedied
By words lovingly spoken.

Sometimes it only takes a few words to mend someone's broken vision…
will you help someone feel better today?

Words

Years and years
I've spent being broken
By words that have been said
Or words that have not been spoken.

I'm sure that I've said my share of things that were hurtful to others, especially to those I love. I just want to say that I'm sorry. We should all be held accountable for the hurtful things we say to each other. Those words can linger inside of us and transfer generationally, creating the same heartbreak over and over again. Words are choices we make. It's never too late...won't you say something encouraging to someone today?

Forgiveness

I hide so much about my own life, about my own hardships and struggles. But there are struggles in my life that have been created from generational pasts - those things that were held on to and passed down. It's not that I hold anyone responsible for my life or my life's choices, but I do see a reflection of yesterday repeating itself. I often ask myself what can I do to change the course or repetition. How can I change how I love myself and how can I show love to others differently?

I think a lot about forgiveness, because I've been told that if I forgive I will be blessed with opportunities to move forward. Yet it seems that no one truly forgives. The past keeps repeating itself. No matter how much you ask others for forgiveness, is it really truly given? There's always a reminder of something that happened; always a reminder of trust that was broken. There are reminders of how yesterday has impacted today. But you have to keep striving to reach a level of forgiveness within yourself and toward others that helps you to move on.

It seems just saying you're sorry isn't enough. Sometimes saying I forgive you isn't enough either. The one thing I do know is that God has forgiven me for so much that I can't even put those things on paper. The list would be unending.

So what is the solution? How do we truly forgive even when the past repeats itself? How do you achieve getting over hurt and pain from years ago and moving into your new season of freedom from the past? How do you get freedom from those things that keep you bound, those things that keep you from living your life as though you really do enjoy being here?

Right now, ask yourself, who are you loving improperly? What are you passing down? Who do you need to forgive? And then, with the best you have in this moment, give them a gift of forgiveness, which is really a gift for you.

I am working very hard to forgive myself for my past, and to forgive others. I am also working very hard to forgive those who have not allowed themselves to forgive me too.

"...clothe yourselves with
compassion, kindness, humility, gentleness and patience.
Bear with each other and forgive one another
if any of you has a grievance against someone.
Forgive as the Lord forgave you. And over all these virtues put on
love, which binds them all together in perfect unity."

Colossians 3:12-13 (NIV)

Forgiving Myself

Sometimes I forget,
Sometimes I don't.
Sometimes I try
But then sometimes I won't.
It's things I remember
And even record.
I'm having trouble
Handing them over to the Lord.
Reminders of personal pain,
A feeling of being lost
And regretful of how much time it cost.
What is it about remembering
That I seem to hold tight
Knowing that letting go is the key to making the past right?
Forgiving myself hasn't been easy for me
So I write down on paper
What I remember
To set myself free!

I'll keep writing my way through,
and one day I will forget to remember.

"The Lord is compassionate and gracious,
slow to anger, abounding in love.
He will not always accuse,
nor will he harbor his anger forever;
he does not treat us as our sins deserve
or repay us according to our iniquities.
For as high as the heavens are above the earth,
so great is his love for those who fear him;
as far as the east is from the west,
so far has he removed our transgressions from us."

Psalm 103:8-12 (NIV)

Just Like Me

With a smile on your face
When you walk through the door,
But truly inside
Something eats at your core.
We sit down and we listen to what's being said
But forget what we've heard before going to bed.
So we start our days over again and again,
Praying forgiveness for all of our sins.
It isn't just me,
I know it's you too,
But we keep on pushing
Until we push through.
So we all must remember
There is truth in what we see.
Someone is feeling
Just like me.
At some point in life
We experience the same
And reach to God for relief from the pain.
So when you go through it
Remember what you see
And help someone else, like you and like me.

Set Your Clock Back

Do you remember
What time it was?
What day it was
You called on God to help you?
Do you remember getting on your knees
And begging God to see you through?
Did you make a promise to fulfill a contract?
Then get mad at God and take your promise back?
But what if God got mad?
And left you all alone?
What if He made broken promises
And left you on your own?
What if the clock that tells your time
Was broken and timeless
Without a God for you to find?
Often times we make promises
We don't keep,
But in times of trouble
It's always God we seek.

I made so many promises to God that if He helped me through situations I would get myself together. I promised I would stop drinking. I promised I would stop smoking. I promised I would stop having sex with men who had no place in my life. I would be a better me.

I kept none of those promises. Over and over again I broke the same promises...I now realize it was myself I let down the most. I am trying harder to keep my promises now and I'm making progress!

The Truth About Me

So what if I told you that I have experienced depression to the point that I wanted to quit? And that on some days I almost did. I almost did. I would even ask God to find someone else to finish being me because I was done being myself.

What if told you that I have anxieties that create great fears in me and that I feel useless at times?

What if I told you that I didn't trust to the point that I have missed out on love, healthy relationships, and loving myself too?

What if I told you that I was tired of being strong and that most of me was broken?

What if I told you that I feel alone even when I'm with others?

What if I told you that I haven't figured out what my purpose is, that I have been searching and trying to fit in, but nothing seems to be my place?

What if I told you that I'm afraid of dreaming because I know when I wake up my reality isn't dreamy at all?

What if I told you that I've spent most of my life trying to figure out what I could have done to be a better daughter so that I felt more loved by my mother in order to reflect love better to others?

What if I told you that at the age of 16 I had a guy hit me in the mouth so hard that I had to have surgery and teeth removed? That I never liked my smile after that, so I got gold teeth to cover up my pain and my frown?

What if I told you that I should have been a better mother to my own children and I'm continuously trying to make up for the breakage in relationships?

What if told you that I've used sex to accommodate me throughout my life?

What if I told you "Hi, my name is Felecia and I'm a recovering sex addict" and that people laugh at me when I tell them I'm 3 years sex-free?

What if I told you I stayed in a physical and verbally abusive relationship because I valued his money more than myself?

What if I told you I went out to the nightclub and left with a guy only to end up being raped. But I just accepted and never spoke about it because I blamed myself more than him.

What if I told you that I tried to commit suicide by taking pills afterwards, but somehow I woke up and went about the next day as if nothing had happened? No one even noticed my pain.

And just what if I told you that it has taken me years to finally have the courage to acknowledge myself, to acknowledge my fears and to ask God for help?

When you allow others to know the truth about you sometimes they can turn away from you, stop loving you, question you, make you feel useless, worthless. They can make you feel like your "what if's" don't matter...it's exhausting.

The one thing I regret in my life is that I waited so long to appreciate myself. That I waited so long to realize that I am here for a reason no matter the "what if's" I have to tell.

So what if I told you that today I am determined!

What if I told you that I am finally getting to a place of understanding my own value.

And what if I told you that I asked God to show my purpose to me and to help me reach it.

That's my new "what ifs"!

Look at Me

I remember when I was a kid,
I wanted to live my life.
But back then I had a different mind
And never thought of wrong or right.
I put myself in places
I knew I shouldn't have been,
And now I seem to revisit
Back then and back when.
Getting high, spirits low
At the blink of my eye
My life could go.
I often look back
And wonder, you know
How much further
My life would go.
And how many things do we use
To keep us on our feet,
All along getting hooked
On daily repeats.

All of the things that keep us bound,
Keep our souls hostage to the ground.
You can't get up,
You won't give up,
Cause now you see
Life has gotten messed up.
You can't catch up,
The devil won't let up.
Now you can't keep your head up
And it's harder for you to cover it up.

How many more tears do you cry?
How often do you ask God why?
When will it break?
What will it take?
What do you do
When Satan comes for you?
When he pulls at your life
Every day and every night,
When he tugs and tears
More than you can bear?
He chains you down,
Locks your soul to the ground.

He can break your will,
Rip your life apart,
And even take ownership
Of your heart.
So I ask you one question,
I ask you to look at me.
Do you see the truth of my hell?
Or that from hell
I have broken free!

Struggle

I don't struggle with wrong or right
But I struggle with trusting God to change my night.
I don't struggle with taking a stand
But I struggle with holding God's hand.
I don't struggle with an evil mind
But I struggle with faith and walking blind.
I don't struggle with a beatless heart
But I struggle with my past and present, keeping them apart.
I don't struggle with opening my eyes
But I struggle with asking God questions like, why?
Eventually I bring myself to believe
That my struggles are for a better me.

To be honest and truthful, every struggle, every problem I've had, if it were not for Jesus I would not have made it through. It's important that we don't give up while we are in our struggles...God is there even when it seems He is not.

Expectations

What we prepare with our minds,
Seeking something we can't find,
So we have no choice but to wait,
And hope that it's not too late.
No need for searching too far...
You are here,
Here you are!

It's my SELF I've been looking for...finally here I am!

Just Thinking

What you think about for one second
Can stop you in your tracks.
It can make you go forward
Or it can make you go back.
So refresh your thinking
It may determine where you go.
Your thinking has the power to convince you
More than your mind
Thinks it knows.

We are what we think,
so encourage your mind to wonder, not wander.

It's 4:53

It's 4:53.
I awake from my sleep.
There are words in my heart
I must write
I must keep.
So I reach for my pen
And paper to write.
Once again I am writing
In the dark
With no light.

Yes, it's true...I write in the dark...I see better there!

Eyes Wide Shut

If I close my eyes
Then I won't see
But with my heart
God shows to me
The way I should follow
Direction from the Son.
I won't look back
Until victory is won.
If my vision is blurred
Or I lose my way,
I will move forward
Each step as I pray,
And even if
My eyes don't see,
With eyes wide shut
God sees for me!

Even when I was blinded by my troubles,
God was seeing for me.

The Little Ant

If an ant can carry loads greater than he
Then what is the difference
Between the ant and me?
The difference is simple,
Unlike the ant
That you see,
While I carry my loads
God is carrying me.

One day I was sitting outside, and I noticed this little ant with such a great load on its back. I said to myself, "Wow, if the ant can do that, I can too!"

Sunlight

Sometimes a sunny day
Doesn't mean you have sunlight.
Sometimes it may mean
In the dark you have sight.
Sometimes when you can't
See anything at all,
Mercy and grace catches you
Before you fall.

Lord knows I've stumbled many times.
I'm glad that mercy and grace were there to catch me!

Irreplaceable You

Be confident about where you are headed.
Always do your best
So that you don't regret it.
While footsteps go away
Because they are erasable,
God has you here for a reason
Your life is irreplaceable!

Defeat

At the end of any competition
One wins and one wins defeat.
When you battle with yourself
It's yourself that you beat!

Even in trying to win my battles I found that I could lose if I didn't tell myself that I could win.

I had a better chance of winning with God on my team.

Failure is Not an Option

I know I myself have a goal to meet
And only I can be my own defeat.
It's not enough to please another someone.
If I fail in the process
Then my own defeat has won.
So I make it no option
To give up on myself.
It must come from me
And not from anyone else.

If I change my heart, I can change my mind too!

Implanted

It's sad that some women
Don't see beauty in themselves.
Hijacking their bodies for ransom
Only to enrich somebody else.
Careful of letting the mirror define you
Instead of implanted illusions.
Stay real and be true, be you.

You're amazing! Embrace who you are.

Irresponsibilities

It amazes me how we say love and don't take the time to show it.
How we say those 4 letters but those we love don't know it.
It's not having someone to hold
Or someone to lay next to
When your skin gets cold.
It's not a conversation
About wrong or right.
It's knowing you can trust
No matter time of day,
No matter time of night.
It's not the laughter
You hear in your ears,
It's the ability to be honest
While crying out your tears.
The ability to show compassion
And understanding from your heart,
While someone else's heart
Has been torn apart.

It's not the words that seem correct
But your sincerity and not sending feelings of reject
So many who love to please
Truly miss out on love
Because of irresponsibilities.

Sex, Sweat and Tears

A lot of years
Sweat and tears.
Somebody's weight
Weighing me down.
If for once
I would say no,
Think more of myself
And not be the bottom
For somebody else.

I realize that lying under a man
has nothing to do with me being a happy woman.
HI, MY NAME IS FELECIA...I AM learning to love myself.

Love Me Not

Love me now
Love me not
Or is it that
You just forgot?
Love me now
Love me not
Or is that
I myself forgot?

Don't forget to love yourself while you are loving others.

Lay Yo'self Down

Lay yo'self down
Rest time is here,
But your mind is still searching
No signs of sleep near.
Tossin' and turnin'
Tomorrow is soon
But you can't close your eyes,
A prisoner to the moon.
Lay yo'self down
Yo life needs a rest.
Let go of your pain
You have done your best.

The night comes to an end but it's ok, you can rest now.
God is still awake!

Fear of Love

My greatest fear is not failure,
It's not even that I get weak.
My fear is not getting
The love that I seek.
The comfort of hugs
On a rainy day.
The I LOVE YOU words
To hear you say.
The smile on your face
When I walk in the room,
And when I leave you're still happy
Again will be soon.

But it's a heart felt pain
That aches in my soul,
That there's a chance
I may never know.
With each day that I start
I seek in my heart
And by night I fold my hands.
I kneel and I pray
That GOD will send this loveless fear away,
And soon she will see
That my fear is her fear of loving me.

I'm not afraid to love you anymore!

I Read Verses

I read verses all the time
But still in search
Of peace of mind.
I say "Lord, I do thank you
For what You have done,"
But before my day ends
Another problem has begun.
And I find that I keep asking
"Why do I read?"
A bible that appears to be
No help to me.
A test of my faith,
A weakening heart.
I know if I quit reading
Life will fall apart.
So I'll keep my book close,
Always close to my hand.
On the days that I fall short
Verses help me to stand.

I used to get upset because when I read the Bible I would expect a right now answer, a right now response from God. Well, it doesn't always happen that way, but keep reading. You will get what you are looking for, just like I did.

Testimony

I try to stay strong
So you can't see it.
God has me speak my testimony
So your life won't repeat it!

We have our stories for the purpose of helping each other through situations. We never know who is listening to us. If you can find it in your heart to be honest I would encourage you to be just that, because someone is needing your story to help them through theirs.

Your testimony matters! Don't forget to share it.

Religion without Meaning

I remember when I started going to church. I wanted so badly to be a part of the congregation. I wanted so badly to be a part of this new lifestyle where people were supposed to be loving and kind and helpful. But I didn't find that. I never felt so isolated in my life. I became angry that the church people were unfriendly and judgmental.

I looked like I was from the streets. I had just lost everything after my son's accident and I didn't have anything to even dress up in. But I went to church because I knew I had to get my life together. Unfortunately all I think I got was turned on religion. Look this way, look that way, clicks that don't accept others, so many do's and don'ts that nobody even noticed that I was hanging on by a thread.

I was battling suicidal thoughts and wanted so badly for someone to just see me; that's all I wanted. But instead I slipped right out the door. I tried my best to keep God in my life no matter the unwelcome receptions that I experienced. I'm learning that people have no place to judge me or my salvation.

I also struggled with my mom being a minister, who I thought was blinded to my struggles and silent cries for help. It seemed that it was easier for her to see and understand the pain suffered by others, but not mine. Every day all I wanted was a hug, to hear her say it's going to be ok. But in all of my trials and tests I know that God was there, even if I felt that the church let a sheep, which was me, wander off.

So what is my message? That it is so important that we are not missing people. There is so much on people's minds and a lot to push through. Sometimes people are in a life or death situation. Their soul has fallen into a dark place. Hopelessness and separation can be a person's last cry for help, so please, don't miss anyone. People are passing by us for a reason. If I would be honest with myself I'd admit that I know God has a ministry in me, but my heart has been hardened and broken by the examples I have seen and I'm afraid of failing others like others have failed me. But I also understand that God's will...will be done.

People Like Me

I didn't feel like I fit,
I was the lost sheep.
What happened to the keepers?
'Cause their help is what I seek.
I turned away
And pretended to not care,
Cause it left my heart
Beatless and bare.
But the truth of the matter
Is that I do,
Just not quite sure
Of how to shine through.
Sheltering my feelings
Keeps me protected
From feeling passed over
And feeling neglected.
Are there people like me
Who feel invisible too?
No matter when you're present
People still don't see you.

These word express how I felt when I tried religion inside the church. I left the building but I didn't leave God. I'm glad He didn't leave me either.

Who Do You Touch?

Is it others who feel
The touch of your hand
When a loved one is closer
Struggling to stand?
Is the smile on your face
Warming another's heart,
Or passing up someone
Who's inside torn apart?
Please don't forget to remember
That no matter who you touch,
Someone close to you
Needs your touch
Just as much.

Don't forget to remember the people that are close to you.
They need you too.

Sow What

Even though we may grow
At different speeds,
We first must make effort
The planting of our seeds.
It's a wonderful experience
To watch your seeds grow.
SOW WHAT? Are you planting?
Make sure what you sow.

Lord, I'm trying, I promise, I'm trying!

Speed of Life

Slow down to appreciate
Life under the sky.
You could pass by yourself
If you pass yourself by.

Try not to miss out on life
because your presence is a blessing to life under the sky!

Her Reflection

You've got to get up, girl, and enter yourself into the world!

She looks in the mirror and instead of noticing her beauty she only notices that things are missing. Things like her smile, her presence, the hope in her eyes, it's all missing. But that's ok, because she can fix herself up, make herself up, cover herself up, dress herself up, and maybe, just maybe, no one will notice that she's not up at all. Such a pretty picture when she's done. Nobody knows she's broken because she looks all put together. No one sees the tiny pieces of pain and hurt that hide underneath.

If she continues through the day and adds just a simple prayer she starts to believe that she can make it through. Keeping all of her pieces together, she makes it!! She survives the day and knows it's time to prepare for another....Lord willing, she says it'll be better.

But before she goes to bed she stands in front of the mirror to take off all of the things that she put on to cover up what was missing in the first place. But there is a difference in what she sees in the mirror this time... she sees God standing there by her reflection.

Don't forget to look in the mirror...there is so much for you to see.

Mirrors

When you look in the mirror
And your reflection is gone
Because something in life
Has gone all wrong.
Took away your presence
And somehow you went missin'
Cause you're stuck in your past
Of broken and it needs fixin'.
What is it about
When you've slipped away?
Gone absent from the present
And holding to yesterday.
There's nothing behind you
But you won't let go,
Afraid of the unknown
Afraid of tomorrow.
What choice will you make?
The mirror is waiting.
Your reflection is needed
For your life of recreating.

It is so very important to not be afraid of tomorrows.
God is already there waiting for you!

I Will

If I sit down,
Sit down and be still,
I'm worried that I
May lose my will.
The will to be strong,
The will to let go,
The will to let God
He sees and He knows.
The will to stand straight,
The will to be great,
The will to remember,
God's never too late.
The will to protect,
The will to redirect,
The will to keep praying,
The will to keep saying
My prayers.
So I'll keep on standing
Standing until
My prayers are answered.
Until then
I will.

I can, and I will.

Trees

I like trees.
They stand strong
Through it all.
I like trees
It takes a lot to make them fall.
I like trees
Because they stand strong.
They reach out into the world
Like God's arms are long.

Even when the trees' leaves change
And they dry up and fall
The tree stands through seasons,
It stands through it all.
The roots are the key
Because they grasp the earth,
And with each new season
A weathered tree will rebirth.

You see, I really do like trees.
And did you know that I am just like a tree?
The Bible tells me so in Psalms 1:3

And he shall be like a tree planted by the rivers of water,
that bringeth forth his fruit in his season; his leaf also shall not wither;
and whatsoever he doeth shall prosper.

Psalm 1:3

In the Middle

Left of me
Right of me
In the middle of my self.
Searching for direction
Trying to be my own help.
Is happiness meant for me?
Can I be unbroken and set free?
Let me pull myself together
And let life be.
Let life be
Happy for me!

I had to figure out what direction I was going so I looked up to God
and trusted that He would get me where I wanted to be – Happy!

Happy!

A happy heart is a beating start.
A beating heart is a happy start.
Somewhere between beats
I just want to be happy!

There's never going to be a perfect life or a perfect me,
but imperfections can bring happiness too!

Pictures

Because I don't take pictures
Doesn't mean that I forget
All the moments that I spent loving
And all the moments that I regret.
I remember my memories differently,
They are etched inside my heart
The memories captured without pictures
Are closer than they are apart.

I wished I had taken more pictures.
But that's ok because I have those times stored in my heart.
My heart is full.

To my children and grandchildren: take lots of pictures!

Interlude

As I type I'm listening to inspirational music. My son's favorite song is playing, "Never Would Have Made It" by Marvin Sapp. It reminds me of all the moments that I made it through. It reminds me of all the times I wanted to give up, but didn't. There's no way I could have done it on my own. I can look back at some of the darkest places in my life and knowingly without a doubt say that God was there with me.

I truly understand that in order to have victory, you have to battle something. In struggles, in moments of despair and hopelessness, if you just keep holding on you will be victorious. We shouldn't compare ourselves to others because we are given our own journey, our own specific encounters and tests so that when tomorrow comes we will be able to look back and know without question that God was working many miracles out for us up ahead in order for us to reach our destinations safely. I'm so thankful.

Every page I have written has been a true and honest feeling from my heart, but of everything that I write, the most important of all is that you must not give up no matter what. You must keep going. What appears to be isn't. Satan has a way of planting props along the way to discourage us. To stop us from winning. To stop us from being happy. To separate us from our course. To destroy our families. To isolate us from our own lives. To keep us in the dark.....and I am thankful to God for giving to me the light that I needed to write in the dark. So now I have one question. Do you understand the meaning of the title?

I'm so grateful. Thank you Lord!

She Has a Chance

Raise her up like the sun when the morning comes
And teach her to smile, to embrace, live life, and have fun.
Encourage her heart to beat like a drum
And don't stop til the day is done.
To be strong within herself and not to be like anyone else.
Teach her where love comes from,
About God our Father and the Son.
Cheer for her accomplishments when she looks your way.
Empower her by teaching her to pray.
Model to her all the strength within and
That if she falls to get up again and again.
Teach her that her journey will be blessed,
That her imperfection is perfection at its best.
And when tears fall down her face
Tell her she's covered in favor, mercy and grace.
To live happily
To be hopeful, joyful and free.
Let her know that she counts
And that being herself is what life is about.
Lift her up! Help her soar to the sky!
Keep her in your prayers, help her to realize
That she's beautiful and precious, to follow God's plans.
Breathe life into her soul so that she has a chance.

I pray every day that a new cycle of love will rebirth into my beautiful daughter and granddaughter. Rikki and Muffin, I love you so much. Love each other with all your hearts. Never let a moment go by without expressing and showing love to each other.

Lost and Found

I'm just a common person
With a goal on my mind
But for some reason
I find myself is hard to find.
Desires and visions,
Accomplishing great things,
But procrastination and doubting
Of what my own power brings.

Something inside keeps me burning like fire
It's my heart telling me to
Fulfill my desire.
So I hope for myself
And believe it to come true,
That by finding myself
I will break myself through!

How much time have I spent creating ideas of something I wanted to do, but let myself talk me out of doing it? Ask yourself, what is it that you would like to do...and do it! You may find that you weren't lost after all. Dream!

Kevi, dream! Grandma loves you very much.
You can do anything you want
because you are predestined for greatness!

Smile!!!

A smile is a movement
We make with our face.
A reminder to the world
Of Gods' mercy and grace.
It's silent, it's bold, a priceless treasure.
A moment of great sharing
Beyond that of great measure.
So what would you do
If one's smile went away
Would you help them to find it?
Or just pass through their day?

I try to look beyond the smiles that I see on faces
because I understand how it feels to be in dark places…alone. Without
anyone noticing that you're not smiling at all.

Moving

I woke up this morning
With a smile on my face,
So thankful for new doses
Of God's mercy and grace.
I know there will be obstacles
But I am not afraid.
The day is what I make it
My joy is not for trade.
If I give up and accept
What could be my defeat,
Then I will miss out
On the victory for me.

It's a daily choice we have to make. But for every day we make it, we can be proud of ourselves for making the right choice.
Make sure to choose yourself today.

Make It Better

This is a reminder to not forget yourself today. A reminder to appreciate yourself for who you are. None of us have it all together; it just looks that way. Figure out what things bring you joy, surround yourself with them. Then figure out what things take away your happiness and remove those things.

Life is short. We never know when the tick tock is going to stop for us or someone we love. My mission is to somehow try to recover a little bit of lost time with people that I love. It is important to me that I give love another chance. Then all of the things from yesterday will eventually no longer have a place in my now or my tomorrows.

I would like to encourage everyone to join me in this recovery process. Life isn't perfect and love isn't either, but in any imperfection there is always an opportunity to make something better.

Don't look at the clock without telling someone you love them today.

Do You Agree with Me?

Nothing really matters if the wrong thing matters.

How do you change a past of hurting when the future looks the same?

What one sees in the eyes is a reflection of what lives in the soul.

If I believed in man more than I believed in God my life would be full of impossibilities, but because I believe in God more than I believe in man anything in my life is possible.

It's no secret that everyone is storing something on the inside from yesterday, so when you say you forgive please do it fully.

What's broken can be repaired as long as you still have all the pieces.

At least 1 person in your day is ready to give up.

Our testimonies should be used to encourage others. So speak up and help someone through their struggles instead of pretending to be perfect.

Do You See What I Write?

There are visions of things
That I keep in my head.
I could probably draw them
But I write them instead.
It's a canvas of expression
To read as an illusion
And the words will create
My heart felt conclusion.
With the stroke of my pen
I write my own art.
Like a painter I'm drawing
But writing from my heart.
I write what I see
In the dark of the night.
Can you see what I'm drawing?
Do you see what I write?

Thank you for taking time to read my canvas.

Laughing

Sometimes I laugh,
Not because something's funny,
But because of how God
Turns my dark into sunny.
Sometimes I laugh
And I may shake my head,
But it's because I'm grateful
For my life, I'm here,
I'm not dead.
So if you see me laughing
Say a quick prayer for me
And ask God to bless
My life with victory!

Pray for me...I'm going to be praying for you too!

ENDNOTES

Message from the Author

You

You can find yourself! That happy place in your life is reachable.

You are the best "you" that there is; don't trade it for anything. Don't go searching for perfection. Learn to appreciate the imperfections that you have been given because that's what makes you who you are. You don't have to convince anyone of your existence. If it appears that you are being missed, passed over, just remember that you're not. We are never alone. Don't question yourself or your abilities. You can achieve anything that you set your heart to. Whatever road you travel just make sure to say your prayers as you journey. Make sure you love yourself. Whatever secrets you hold from yesterday, send them floating up to the sky so that the heavens can turn them into new dreams. And don't forget to remember to thank God for keeping you here through it all!

Family

I want to acknowledge my family. I want to say thank you for doing your best. I appreciate being a part of the family that God has assigned me to. Each one of you has your own story, and we are blessed to have each other. Sometimes we get so busy that family time gets less and less but I always knew that you were there.

My story is about my own struggles and how I wrote to keep myself here when I thought I'd go crazy from trying to maintain my presence. It's a funny thing that those who are closest to us are the ones we don't reach out to. However, on June 25, 2005, a Friday night when I felt so alone and so helpless, I remember that you, my family, were there for me. Little by little something happened inside of me that I never recovered from. My heart seemed to change that day. I was afraid for my son's life, watching his life slip away. I don't know what I would have done without you there at that moment, in that place, I would not have made it without you.

To my beautiful daughter Rikki, I say thank you for taking care of your mother unconditionally. I don't know what I would have done without you at that moment, in that place. I would not have made it without you. You inspire me more than you know. You are powerful and stronger than I am. Thank you Rikki again for being there for me.

To my miracle son Mikey, I always tell you that you saved my life. It's true! What happened that night was the worst thing that ever happened to me, but it was also the best thing that happened because my life needed to change and probably would not have without something happening just like it did. I begged God's forgiveness because He had been trying to get my attention for so long and I just kept living my way.

It's amazing how God has things put into place for His own purpose. All of the people and the perfect timing it took to get us all through that horrible night. Thank you to everyone who came to the hospital and prayed.

After awhile, God started spending personal time with me in the hospital. I could feel His presence late at night. I'd awake and I could hear His voice giving me instructions, as if He were there, right there with me. It was then my heart led me to remove my gold teeth, to remove all of the junk I used to cover myself up with. God was getting me back to being Felecia. I had to let go of the girl I saw in the mirror in order for me to see a new reflection. It was just the beginning to my new life, the beginning to me truly finding out who God was; who I was and what my purpose was. Life was falling into place again! It was an experience that without having it I may not have lived to tell my story. I'm glad I made it!

Thank you to my family and to everyone who helped me along the way. I appreciate your presence in my life! Life is looking up now and I think I'm finally getting my past behind me!

Family isn't chosen by us...we are each handpicked by the Potter to serve a purpose for each other. Don't forget to love those assigned to your family – imperfections and all!

Thankfulness

Hi, my name is Felecia, and I want to say thank you Lord for sticking with me! I write in the dark but you have been my light through it all!

Rikki, Muffin, Ayce, Mikey, Kevi, I love you and I'm proud of you too! Be the best you that you can be, love a lot and let God lead the way!! Don't be afraid to live, take chances and when you make mistakes, pray and ask God to guide your way. Know that each of you is amazing and capable of your hearts' desires. Support and love each other unconditionally at all times. Life is waiting for you, go and be happy!

Today I celebrate being free from my sex addiction for 3 years. It's been a wonderful time, refreshing and renewing. I understand that the removal of sex in my life has allowed me to get closer to God, appreciate myself, love myself, and truly understand that I am worth it. That my purpose in life is waiting for me just on the other side of my fears. When my life is positioned for a loving relationship, God will let me know, but for now I'm enjoying the new me. Today I am also celebrating 10 years of being free from the streets. I am saved by God's mercy, grace, and forgiveness.

I gave my life to Christ on Friday, June 25, 2005. That was the night I made promises to God to live better if my son's life was spared. I am still keeping my promises, Lord! I am going to keep doing my best! Thank you, Lord, for allowing me to write this book, for being my light, while **I Write in the dark**, and for letting my truths be told.

Your Word is a lamp to my feet
And a light for my path.

Psalm 119:105 (NIV)

The desire to write this book has never been about me. My prayer is that after reading it, someone will live life more free! Yet every word that I have written helped me make it through the night.

And I now know that...

I am writing
IN THE LIGHT!

About the Author

Felecia Marie Wellington is a passionate woman who recently left a job of 25 years after praying to God for her purpose to be revealed. Within a week her 93-year-old grandmother needed home-care and that's where her purpose was revealed. While caring for her grandmother she was inspired to create Mirror Ministry, a ministry that encourages women to believe in their purpose and their beauty. Felecia walks the streets to engage with the community in hopes of passing along the same hope she received from God to others. Stepping out in faith was her challenge but it also helped Felecia find her way to her purpose.

In her time alone she enjoys art and music, mixed with lots of prayer. She is a mother of 2 amazing children and 3 very cool and wonderful grandchildren. She resides in Indianapolis, Indiana.

*Piecing our pieces together
isn't always easy,
but it is the only way
we will ever find the peace that we need
to truly be happy.*

Peace your pieces together!

Don't forget to remember
someone needs our love today.

Let us each do better about
how we love ourselves and each other!

Made in the USA
San Bernardino, CA
08 December 2015